A Note to Parents

DK READERS is a compelling program for beginning readers, designed in conjunction with leading literacy experts, including Dr. Linda Gambrell, Distinguished Professor of Education at Clemson University. Dr. Gambrell has served as President of the National Reading Conference, the College Reading Association, and the International Reading Association.

Beautiful illustrations and superb full-color photographs combine with engaging, easy-to-read stories to offer a fresh approach to each subject in the series. Each DK READER is guaranteed to capture a child's interest while developing his or her reading skills, general knowledge, and love of reading.

The five levels of DK READERS are aimed at different reading abilities, enabling you to choose the books that are exactly right for your child:

Pre-level 1: Learning to read
Level 1: Beginning to read
Level 2: Beginning to read alone
Level 3: Reading alone
Level 4: Proficient readers

The "normal" age at which a child begins to read can be anywhere from three to eight years old. Adult participation through the lower levels is very helpful for providing encouragement, discussing storylines, and sounding out unfamiliar words.

No matter which level you select, you can be sure that you are helping your child learn to read, then read to learn!

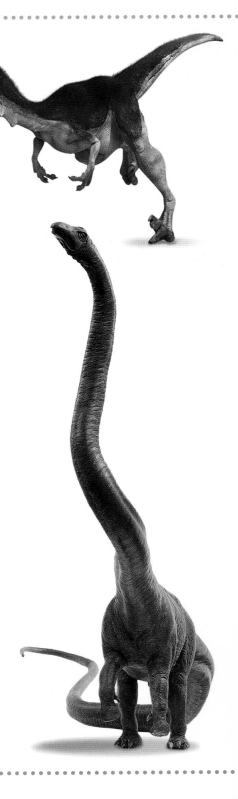

**LONDON, NEW YORK, MUNICH,
DELHI, AND MELBOURNE**

Project Editor Mary Atkinson
Art Editor Karen Lieberman
Senior Editor Linda Esposito
Deputy Managing Art Editor Jane Horne
Publishing Manager Bridget Giles
US Editor Regina Kahney
Production Editor Marc Staples
Picture Researcher Mary Sweeney
Scientific Consultant Dr. Angela Milner

Reading Consultant
Linda B. Gambrell, Ph.D.

First American Edition, 1998
This edition, 2011
11 12 13 14 15 16 10 9 8 7 6 5 4 3 2 1
Published in the United States by DK Publishing
375 Hudson Street, New York, New York 10014

Published in Great Britain by Dorling Kindersley Limited.

DK books are available at special discounts when purchased in bulk
for sales promotions, premiums, fund-raising, or educational use.
For details, contact: DK Publishing Special Markets
375 Hudson Street, New York, New York 10014
SpecialSales@dk.com

A catalog record for this book is available
from the Library of Congress

ISBN: 978-0-7566-7586-8 (pb)
ISBN: 978-0-7566-7585-1 (plc)

Color reproduction by Printing LTD
Printed and bound in China by L Rex Printing Co., Ltd.

The publisher would like to thank the following:
Museums: Natural History Museum, London, and Royal Tyrrel
Museum of Palaeontolgy, Alberta
Artists/model makers: Roby Braun, Jim Channell, John Holmes,
Graham High/Jeremy Hunt/Centaur Studios, and Kenneth Lilly
Photographers: Andy Crawford, John Downs,
Neil Fletcher, Dave King, Tim Ridley, and Dave Rudkin.**Jacket
images:** *Front:* **Dorling Kindersley:** Jon Hughes.

All other images © Dorling Kindersley.
For further information see: www.dkimages.com

Discover more at
www.dk.com

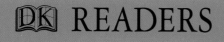

DK READERS

BEGINNING TO READ ALONE 2

Dinosaur Dinners

Written by Lee Davis

DK
DK Publishing

I am a dinosaur
looking for my breakfast.

I can see you,
wherever you are.

A deadly dinosaur
Troodon was a quick
and clever hunter.
It had large eyes for spotting
prey, even in dim light.

Troodon
(TROE-uh-don)

I am a dinosaur
ready for my lunch.

Herrerasaurus
(her-RARE-uh-SORE-us)

I can catch you,
even if you run.

A speedy sprinter
Herrerasaurus ran fast
on its two back legs.
It hunted small reptiles,
such as lizards.

I am a dinosaur,
hungry for my dinner.
And I am bigger than you are.

A huge hunter

Tyrannosaurus was one of
the biggest meat-eating
dinosaurs ever. It was as tall
as a two-story building.

Tyrannosaurus
(tie-RAN-uh-SORE-us)

We all have
sharp teeth and claws.
We are meat eaters.
We eat other dinosaurs.

Tyrannosaurus

Herrerasaurus

Hungry for meat

Meat-eating dinosaurs ate
fish, insects, small mammals,
reptiles, and other dinosaurs.
They are called carnivores.

Eat or be eaten?
That is the dinosaur question.

I can run fast enough to get away
from the big meat eaters.
I can also run fast enough
to catch small animals.

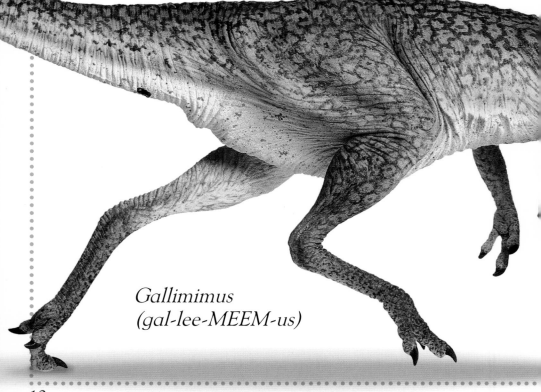

Gallimimus
(gal-lee-MEEM-us)

A mixed diet

Gallimimus snapped up leaves and small animals in its beak. It is called an omnivore because it ate both plants and meat.

I like to eat lizards
and other animals.
I catch them
in my strong claws
and my long beak.
But I eat plants, too.
I am not a picky eater.

I am a dinosaur
who eats nothing but plants.
I stay close to my babies
to protect them from meat eaters.

Maiasaura
(MY-uh-SORE-uh)

Eggs in a nest

Dinosaurs laid eggs in nests on the ground. Their babies hatched out of the eggs, just like baby birds and crocodiles.

I made their nest
from a mound of earth.
I bring leaves and berries
for them to eat.

Dinosaurs that don't eat meat
need protection from those that do.
Our spikes are long and sharp.
If meat eaters come too close,
we take them on head first.

Dinos and rhinos

Styracosaurus had
a long horn on its nose.
It used the horn
for protection,
like the rhinoceros does today.

Styracosaurus
(sty-RAK-uh-SORE-us)

Sharp teeth cannot dent
my body armor.
And watch out for the spikes
on my shoulders.
One bump from me and
it's the end.

Edmontonia
(ed-mon-TONE-ee-uh)

My skin is as hard as a rock.
My body is covered
in studs, spikes, and horns.

I swing the club
on the end of my tail.
It can break the legs
of the bigger dinosaurs.

Euoplocephalus
(you-op-loe-SEF-uh-lus)

Bone-breaking bones

A tail club could grow
as wide as an armchair.
It was a powerful weapon
against meat eaters.

I am not very big,

but I am dangerous.

We are small but fast.
We eat plants that
grow close to the ground.

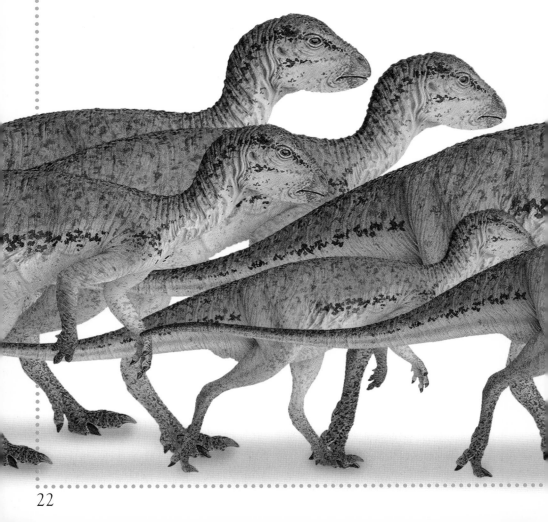

We live in a herd.
If one of us spots a meat eater,
we all zoom off
on our strong back legs.

Hypsilophodon
(hip-si-LOAF-uh-don)

We don't need special weapons.
If we smell danger,
we raise the alarm.
We use our head crests like trumpets
to make loud hooting calls.

Fancy heads

Other dinosaurs had
crests on their heads, too.
Often the males had bigger
crests than the females.

Parasaurolophus
(par-uh-sore-oh-LOAF-us)

Corythosaurus
(koe-rith-uh-SORE-us)

I look frightening
because I am so big.

I need to eat
huge amounts of leaves
to keep myself going.
I use my long neck
to reach the leaves
at the tops of trees.

Barosaurus
(bar-uh-SORE-us)

I can see danger coming
from any direction.
I am much taller
than any of the meat eaters.

We are all dinosaurs that eat plants. We all have some way of protecting ourselves from meat eaters.

Barosaurus

Styracosaurus

Euoplocephalus

Plant lovers

Animals that eat nothing but plants are called herbivores. Most of the dinosaurs were herbivores.

Hypsilophodon

Edmontonia

Corythosaurus

Maiasaura

We are all dinosaurs.
What do we eat for dinner?

Dinosaur glossary

Barosaurus (bar-uh-SORE-us)
- name means "heavy lizard"
- a herbivore (plant eater)
- 89 feet (27 meters) long
- lived 150 million years ago

Corythosaurus (koe-rith-uh-SORE-us)
- name means "helmet lizard"
- a herbivore
- 33 feet (10 meters) long
- lived 75 million years ago

Edmontonia (ed-mon-TONE-ee-uh)
- name means "from Edmonton" (Canada)
- a herbivore
- 23 feet (7 meters) long
- lived 74–72 million years ago

Euoplocephalus (you-op-loe-SEF-uh-lus)
- name means "well-armored head"
- a herbivore
- 23 feet (7 meters) long
- lived 73 million years ago

Gallimimus (gal-lee-MEEM-us)
- name means "chicken mimic"
- an omnivore (plant and meat eater)
- 20 feet (6 meters) long
- lived 73 million years ago

Herrerasaurus (her-RARE-uh-SORE-us)
- name means "Herrera's lizard" after Victorino Herrera who discovered it
- a carnivore (meat eater)
- 10 feet (3 meters) long
- lived 228 million years ago

Hypsilophodon (hip-si-LOAF-uh-don)
- name means "high ridge tooth"
- a herbivore
- 7–8 feet (2–2.5 meters) long
- lived 120 million years ago

Maiasaura (MY-uh-SORE-uh)
- name means "good mother lizard"
- a herbivore
- 30 feet (9 meters) long
- lived 80–75 million years ago

Parasaurolophus (par-uh-sore-oh-LOAF-us)
- name means "beside ridge lizard"
- a herbivore
- 33 feet (10 meters) long
- lived 75–70 million years ago

Styracosaurus (sty-RAK-uh-SORE-us)
- name means "spiked lizard"
- a herbivore
- 18 feet (5.5 meters) long
- lived 75–72 million years ago

Troodon (TROE-uh-don)
- name means "wounding tooth"
- a carnivore
- 6 feet (2 meters) long
- lived 73–65 million years ago

Tyrannosaurus (tie-RAN-uh-SORE-us)
- name means "tyrant lizard"
- a carnivore
- 39 feet (12 meters) long
- lived 67–65 million years ago